Soon To Be Mr. & Mrs.

Wedding Date:

Wedding Planner

WEDDING DATE & TIME:

TO DO LIST:

VENUE ADDRESS:

BUDGET:

OFFICIANT:

WEDDING PARTY:

NOTES & REMINDERS:

Wedding Budget Planner

	TOTAL COST:	DEPOSIT:	REMAINDER:
WEDDING VENUE			
RECEPTION VENUE			
FLORIST			
OFFICIANT			
CATERER			
WEDDING CAKE			
BRIDAL ATTIRE			
GROOM ATTIRE			
BRIDAL JEWELRY			
BRIDESMAID ATTIRE			
GROOMSMEN ATTIRE			
HAIR & MAKE UP			
PHOTOGRAPHER			
VIDEOGRAPHER			
DJ SERVICE/ENTERTAINMENT			
INVITATIONS			
TRANSPORTATION			
WEDDING PARTY GIFTS			
RENTALS			
HONEYMOON			

12 Months Before

SET THE DATE

SET YOUR BUDGET

CHOOSE YOUR THEME

ORGANIZE ENGAGEMENT PARTY

RESEARCH VENUES

BOOK A WEDDING PLANNER

RESEARCH PHOTOGRAPHERS

RESEARCH VIDEOGRAPHERS

RESEARCH DJ'S/ENTERTAINMENT

CONSIDER FLORISTS

RESEARCH CATERERS

DECIDE ON OFFICIANT

CREATE INITIAL GUEST LIST

CHOOSE WEDDING PARTY

SHOP FOR WEDDING DRESS

REGISTER WITH GIFT REGISTRY

DISCUSS HONEYMOON IDEAS

RESEARCH WEDDING RINGS

THINGS TO REMEMBER:

9 Months Before

FINALIZE GUEST LIST	CHOOSE WEDDING GOWN
ORDER INVITATIONS	ORDER BRIDESMAIDS DRESSES
PLAN YOUR RECEPTION	RESERVE TUXEDOS
BOOK PHOTOGRAPHER	ARRANGE TRANSPORTATION
BOOK VIDEOGRAPHER	BOOK WEDDING VENUE
BOOK FLORIST	BOOK RECEPTION VENUE
BOOK DJ/ENTERTAINMENT	PLAN HONEYMOON
BOOK CATERER	BOOK OFFICIANT
CHOOSE WEDDING CAKE	BOOK ROOMS FOR GUESTS

THINGS TO REMEMBER:

6 Months Before

ORDER THANK YOU NOTES	BOOK HAIR/MAKE UP STYLIST
REVIEW RECEPTION DETAILS	CONFIRM MUSIC SELECTIONS
MAKE APPT FOR DRESS FITTING	PLAN BRIDAL SHOWER
CONFIRM BRIDEMAIDS DRESSES	PLAN REHEARSAL
GET MARRIAGE LICENSE	SHOP FOR WEDDING RINGS

THINGS TO REMEMBER:

3 Months Before

MAIL OUT INVITATIONS

MEET WITH OFFICIANT

BUY GIFTS FOR WEDDING PARTY

BOOK FINAL GOWN FITTING

BUY WEDDING BANDS

PLAN YOUR HAIR STYLE

PURCHASE SHOES/HEELS

CONFIRM PASSPORTS ARE VALID

FINALIZE RECEPTION MENU

PLAN REHEARSAL DINNER

CONFIRM ALL BOOKINGS

APPLY FOR MARRIAGE LICENSE

CONFIRM MUSIC SELECTIONS

DRAFT WEDDING VOWS

CHOOSE YOUR MC

ARRANGE AIRPORT TRANSFER

THINGS TO REMEMBER:

1 Month Before

CONFIRM FINAL GUEST COUNT	REHEARSE WEDDING VOWS
CONFIRM RECEPTION DETAILS	BOOK MANI-PEDI
ATTEND FINAL GOWN FITTING	CONFIRM WITH FLORIST
CONFIRM PHOTOGRAPHER	CONFIRM VIDEOGRAPHER
WRAP WEDDING PARTY GIFTS	PICK UP BRIDEMAIDS DRESSES
CREATE PHOTOGRAPHY SHOT LIST	CREATE WEDDING SCHEDULE

THINGS TO REMEMBER:

1 Week Before

FINALIZE SEATING PLANS

MAKE PAYMENTS TO VENDORS

PACK FOR HONEYMOON

CONFIRM HOTEL RESERVATIONS

GIVE SCHEDULE TO PARTY

DELIVER LICENSE TO OFFICIANT

CONFIRM WITH BAKERY

PICK UP WEDDING DRESS

PICK UP TUXEDOS

GIVE MUSIC LIST TO DJ

THINGS TO REMEMBER:

1 Day Before

GET MANICURE/PEDICURE   GIVE GIFTS TO WEDDING PARTY

ATTEND REHEARSAL DINNER   FINALIZE PACKING

GET A GOOD NIGHT'S SLEEP!

TO DO LIST:

The Big Day!

GET HAIR & MAKE UP DONE

HAVE A HEALTHY BREAKFAST

ENJOY YOUR BIG DAY!

MEET WITH BRIDESMAIDS

GIVE RINGS TO BEST MAN

TO DO LIST:

Wedding Planner

ENGAGEMENT PARTY:

DATE:

LOCATION:

TIME:

NUMBER OF GUESTS:

NOTES:

BRIDAL SHOWER:

DATE:

LOCATION:

TIME:

NUMBER OF GUESTS:

NOTES:

STAG & DOE PARTY:

DATE:

LOCATION:

TIME:

NUMBER OF GUESTS:

NOTES:

Wedding Party

MAID/MATRON OF HONOR:

PHONE: DRESS SIZE: SHOE SIZE:

EMAIL:

BRIDESMAID:

PHONE: DRESS SIZE: SHOE SIZE:

EMAIL:

BRIDESMAID #2:

PHONE: DRESS SIZE: SHOE SIZE:

EMAIL:

BRIDESMAID #3:

PHONE: DRESS SIZE: SHOE SIZE:

EMAIL:

BRIDESMAID #4:

PHONE: DRESS SIZE: SHOE SIZE:

EMAIL:

NOTES:

Wedding Party

BEST MAN:

PHONE: WAIST SIZE: SHOE SIZE:

NECK SIZE: SLEEVE SIZE: JACKET SIZE:

EMAIL:

GROOMSMEN #1:

PHONE: WAIST SIZE: SHOE SIZE:

NECK SIZE: SLEEVE SIZE: JACKET SIZE:

EMAIL:

GROOMSMEN #2:

PHONE: WAIST SIZE: SHOE SIZE:

NECK SIZE: SLEEVE SIZE: JACKET SIZE:

EMAIL:

GROOMSMEN #3:

PHONE: WAIST SIZE: SHOE SIZE:

NECK SIZE: SLEEVE SIZE: JACKET SIZE:

EMAIL:

GROOMSMEN #4:

PHONE: WAIST SIZE: SHOE SIZE:

NECK SIZE: SLEEVE SIZE: JACKET SIZE:

EMAIL:

Photographer

PHOTOGRAPHER:

PHONE: COMPANY:

EMAIL: ADDRESS:

WEDDING PACKAGE OVERVIEW:

EST PRICE:

INCLUSIONS:	YES ✓	NO ✓	COST:
ENGAGEMENT SHOOT:			
PHOTO ALBUMS:			
FRAMES:			
PROOFS INCLUDED:			
NEGATIVES INCLUDED:			

TOTAL COST:

Videographer

VIDEOGRAPHER:

PHONE: COMPANY:

EMAIL: ADDRESS:

WEDDING PACKAGE OVERVIEW:

EST PRICE:

INCLUSIONS: YES ✓   NO ✓   COST:

DUPLICATES/COPIES:

PHOTO MONTAGE:

MUSIC ADDED:

EDITING:

TOTAL COST:

NOTES:

DJ/Entertainment

DJ/LIVE BAND/ENTERTAINMENT:

PHONE: COMPANY:

EMAIL: ADDRESS:

START TIME: END TIME:

ENTERTAINMENT SERVICE OVERVIEW:

EST PRICE:

INCLUSIONS:	YES ✓	NO ✓	COST:
SOUND EQUIPMENT:			
LIGHTING:			
SPECIAL EFFECTS:			
GRATUITIES			

TOTAL COST:

NOTES:

Florist

FLORIST:

PHONE: COMPANY:

EMAIL: ADDRESS:

FLORAL PACKAGE:

EST PRICE: _____

INCLUSIONS: YES   ✓   NO   ✓   COST:

BRIDAL BOUQUET:

THROW AWAY BOUQUET:

CORSAGES:

CEREMONY FLOWERS

CENTERPIECES

CAKE TOPPER

BOUTONNIERE

TOTAL COST:

Wedding Cake/Baker

PHONE: COMPANY:

EMAIL: ADDRESS:

WEDDING CAKE PACKAGE:

COST: _____ FREE TASTING: _____ DELIVERY FEE: _____

FLAVOR:

FILLING:

SIZE:

SHAPE:

COLOR:

EXTRAS:

TOTAL COST:

NOTES:

Transportation Planner

TO CEREMONY: PICK UP TIME: PICK UP LOCATION:

BRIDE:

GROOM:

BRIDE'S PARENTS:

GROOM'S PARENTS:

BRIDESMAIDS:

GROOMSMEN:

NOTES:

TO RECEPTION: PICK UP TIME: PICK UP LOCATION:

BRIDE & GROOM:

BRIDE'S PARENTS:

GROOM'S PARENTS:

BRIDESMAIDS:

GROOMSMEN:

Wedding Planner

BACHELORETTE PARTY:

DATE:

LOCATION:

TIME:

NUMBER OF GUESTS:

NOTES:

BACHELOR PARTY:

DATE:

LOCATION:

TIME:

NUMBER OF GUESTS:

NOTES:

CEREMONY REHEARSAL:

DATE:

LOCATION:

TIME:

NUMBER OF GUESTS:

NOTES:

Wedding Planner

REHEARSAL DINNER:

DATE:

LOCATION:

TIME:

NUMBER OF GUESTS:

NOTES:

RECEPTION:

DATE:

LOCATION:

TIME:

NUMBER OF GUESTS:

NOTES:

REMINDERS:

Names & Addresses

CEREMONY:

PHONE:

CONTACT NAME:

EMAIL:

ADDRESS:

RECEPTION:

PHONE:

CONTACT NAME:

EMAIL:

ADDRESS:

OFFICIANT:

PHONE:

CONTACT NAME:

EMAIL:

ADDRESS:

WEDDING PLANNER:

PHONE:

CONTACT NAME:

EMAIL:

ADDRESS:

CATERER:

PHONE:

CONTACT NAME:

EMAIL:

ADDRESS:

FLORIST:

PHONE:

CONTACT NAME:

EMAIL:

ADDRESS:

Names & Addresses

BAKERY:

PHONE: CONTACT NAME:

EMAIL: ADDRESS:

BRIDAL SHOP:

PHONE: CONTACT NAME:

EMAIL: ADDRESS:

PHOTOGRAPHER:

PHONE: CONTACT NAME:

EMAIL: ADDRESS:

VIDEOGRAPHER:

PHONE: CONTACT NAME:

EMAIL: ADDRESS:

DJ/ENTERTAINMENT:

PHONE: CONTACT NAME:

EMAIL: ADDRESS:

HAIR/NAIL SALON:

PHONE: CONTACT NAME:

EMAIL: ADDRESS:

Names & Addresses

MAKE UP ARTIST:

PHONE:

CONTACT NAME:

EMAIL:

ADDRESS:

RENTALS:

PHONE:

CONTACT NAME:

EMAIL:

ADDRESS:

HONEYMOON RESORT/HOTEL:

PHONE:

CONTACT NAME:

EMAIL:

ADDRESS:

TRANSPORTATION SERVICE:

PHONE:

CONTACT NAME:

EMAIL:

ADDRESS:

NOTES:

Caterer Details

CONTACT INFORMATION:

PHONE: CONTACT NAME:

EMAIL: ADDRESS:

MENU CHOICE #1:

MENU CHOICE #2:

YES ✓   NO ✓   COST:

BAR INCLUDED:

CORKAGE FEE:

HORS D'OEUVRES:

TAXES INCLUDED:

GRATUITIES INCLUDED:

Menu Planner

HORS D'OEUVRES

1st COURSE:

2nd COURSE:

3rd COURSE:

4th COURSE:

DESSERT:

1 Week Before

THINGS TO DO: NOTES:

MONDAY

TUESDAY

WEDNESDAY

THURSDAY

REMINDERS & NOTES:

1 Week Before

THINGS TO DO: NOTES:

FRIDAY

SATURDAY

SUNDAY

LEFT TO DO:

REMINDERS: NOTES:

Wedding Guest List

NAME:	ADDRESS:	# IN PARTY:	RSVP: ✓

Wedding Guest List

NAME:	ADDRESS:	# IN PARTY:	RSVP: ✓

Wedding Guest List

NAME:	ADDRESS:	# IN PARTY:	RSVP: ✓

Wedding Guest List

NAME:	ADDRESS:	# IN PARTY:	RSVP: ✓

Wedding Guest List

NAME:	ADDRESS:	# IN PARTY:	RSVP: ✓

Wedding Guest List

NAME:	ADDRESS:	# IN PARTY:	RSVP: ✓

Wedding Guest List

NAME:	ADDRESS:	# IN PARTY:	RSVP: ✓

Wedding Guest List

NAME:	ADDRESS:	# IN PARTY:	RSVP: ✓

Wedding Guest List

NAME:	ADDRESS:	# IN PARTY:	RSVP: ✓

Wedding Guest List

NAME:	ADDRESS:	# IN PARTY:	RSVP: ✓

Wedding Guest List

NAME:	ADDRESS:	# IN PARTY:	RSVP: ✓

Wedding Guest List

NAME:	ADDRESS:	# IN PARTY:	RSVP: ✓

Wedding Guest List

NAME:	ADDRESS:	# IN PARTY:	RSVP: ✓

Wedding Guest List

NAME:	ADDRESS:	# IN PARTY:	RSVP: ✓

Wedding Guest List

NAME:	ADDRESS:	# IN PARTY:	RSVP: ✓

Wedding Guest List

NAME:	ADDRESS:	# IN PARTY:	RSVP: ✓

Wedding Guest List

NAME:	ADDRESS:	# IN PARTY:	RSVP: ✓

Wedding Guest List

NAME:	ADDRESS:	# IN PARTY:	RSVP: ✓

Wedding Guest List

NAME:	ADDRESS:	# IN PARTY:	RSVP: ✓

Wedding Guest List

NAME:	ADDRESS:	# IN PARTY:	RSVP: ✓

Wedding Guest List

NAME:	ADDRESS:	# IN PARTY:	RSVP: ✓

Wedding Guest List

NAME:	ADDRESS:	# IN PARTY:	RSVP: ✓

Wedding Guest List

NAME:	ADDRESS:	# IN PARTY:	RSVP: ✓

Wedding Guest List

NAME:	ADDRESS:	# IN PARTY:	RSVP: ✓

Wedding Guest List

NAME:	ADDRESS:	# IN PARTY:	RSVP: ✓

Wedding Guest List

NAME:	ADDRESS:	# IN PARTY:	RSVP: ✓

Wedding Guest List

NAME:	ADDRESS:	# IN PARTY:	RSVP: ✓

Wedding Guest List

NAME:	ADDRESS:	# IN PARTY:	RSVP: ✓

Wedding Guest List

NAME:	ADDRESS:	# IN PARTY:	RSVP: ✓

Wedding Guest List

NAME:	ADDRESS:	# IN PARTY:	RSVP: ✓

Wedding Guest List

NAME:	ADDRESS:	# IN PARTY:	RSVP: ✓

Wedding Guest List

NAME:	ADDRESS:	# IN PARTY:	RSVP: ✓

Wedding Guest List

NAME:	ADDRESS:	# IN PARTY:	RSVP: ✓

Wedding Guest List

NAME:	ADDRESS:	# IN PARTY:	RSVP: ✓

Wedding Guest List

NAME:	ADDRESS:	# IN PARTY:	RSVP: ✓

Wedding Guest List

NAME:	ADDRESS:	# IN PARTY:	RSVP: ✓

Wedding Guest List

NAME:	ADDRESS:	# IN PARTY:	RSVP: ✓

Wedding Guest List

NAME:	ADDRESS:	# IN PARTY:	RSVP: ✓

Wedding Guest List

NAME:	ADDRESS:	# IN PARTY:	RSVP: ✓

Wedding Guest List

NAME:	ADDRESS:	# IN PARTY:	RSVP: ✓

Wedding Guest List

NAME:	ADDRESS:	# IN PARTY:	RSVP: ✓

Wedding Guest List

NAME:	ADDRESS:	# IN PARTY:	RSVP: ✓

Wedding Guest List

NAME:	ADDRESS:	# IN PARTY:	RSVP: ✓

Wedding Guest List

NAME:	ADDRESS:	# IN PARTY:	RSVP: ✓

Wedding Guest List

NAME:	ADDRESS:	# IN PARTY:	RSVP: ✓

Wedding Guest List

NAME:	ADDRESS:	# IN PARTY:	RSVP: ✓

Seating Chart Planner

Table #

Table #

Table #

Table #

SEATING PLANNER NOTES:

Seating Chart Planner

Table #

Table #

Table #

Table #

SEATING PLANNER NOTES:

Seating Chart Planner

Table #

Table #

Table #

Table #

SEATING PLANNER NOTES:

Seating Chart Planner

Table #

Table #

Table #

Table #

SEATING PLANNER NOTES:

Seating Chart Planner

Table #

Table #

Table #

Table #

SEATING PLANNER NOTES:

Seating Chart Planner

Table #

Table #

Table #

Table #

SEATING PLANNER NOTES:

Seating Chart Planner

Table #

Table #

Table #

Table #

SEATING PLANNER NOTES:

Seating Chart Planner

Table #

Table #

Table #

Table #

SEATING PLANNER NOTES:

Seating Chart Planner

Table #

Table #

Table #

Table #

SEATING PLANNER NOTES:

Seating Chart Planner

Table #

Table #

Table #

Table #

SEATING PLANNER NOTES:

Seating Chart Planner

Table #

Table #

Table #

Table #

SEATING PLANNER NOTES:

Seating Chart Planner

Table #

Table #

Table #

Table #

SEATING PLANNER NOTES:

Seating Chart Planner

Table #

Table #

Table #

Table #

SEATING PLANNER NOTES:

Seating Chart Planner

Table #   Table #

Table #   Table #

SEATING PLANNER NOTES:

Seating Chart Planner

Table #

Table #

Table #

Table #

SEATING PLANNER NOTES:

Seating Chart Planner

Table #

Table #

Table #

Table #

SEATING PLANNER NOTES:

Seating Chart Planner

Table #

Table #

Table #

Table #

SEATING PLANNER NOTES:

Seating Chart Planner

Table #

Table #

Table #

Table #

SEATING PLANNER NOTES:

Seating Chart Planner

Table #

Table #

Table #

Table #

SEATING PLANNER NOTES:

Seating Chart Planner

Table #

Table #

Table #

Table #

SEATING PLANNER NOTES:

Seating Chart Planner

Table #

Table #

Table #

Table #

SEATING PLANNER NOTES:

Seating Chart Planner

Table #

Table #

Table #

Table #

SEATING PLANNER NOTES:

Seating Chart Planner

Table #

Table #

Table #

Table #

SEATING PLANNER NOTES:

Seating Chart Planner

Table #

Table #

Table #

Table #

SEATING PLANNER NOTES:

Seating Chart Planner

Table #

Table #

Table #

Table #

SEATING PLANNER NOTES:

Seating Chart Planner

Table #

Table #

Table #

Table #

SEATING PLANNER NOTES:

Seating Chart Planner

Table #

Table #

Table #

Table #

SEATING PLANNER NOTES:

Seating Chart Planner

Table #

Table #

Table #

Table #

SEATING PLANNER NOTES:

Seating Chart Planner

Table #

Table #

Table #

Table #

SEATING PLANNER NOTES:

Seating Chart Planner

Table #

Table #

Table #

Table #

SEATING PLANNER NOTES:

Seating Chart Planner

Table #

Table #

Table #

Table #

SEATING PLANNER NOTES:

Seating Chart Planner

Table #

Table #

Table #

Table #

SEATING PLANNER NOTES:

Seating Chart Planner

Table #

Table #

Table #

Table #

Seating Chart Planner

Table #

Table #

Table #

Table #

SEATING PLANNER NOTES:

Seating Chart Planner

Table #

Table #

Table #

Table #

SEATING PLANNER NOTES:

Seating Chart Planner

Table #

Table #

Table #

Table #

SEATING PLANNER NOTES:

Seating Chart Planner

Table #

Table #

Table #

Table #

SEATING PLANNER NOTES:

Seating Chart Planner

Table #

Table #

Table #

Table #

SEATING PLANNER NOTES:

Seating Chart Planner

Table #

Table #

Table #

Table #

SEATING PLANNER NOTES:

Seating Chart Planner

Table #

Table #

Table #

Table #

SEATING PLANNER NOTES:

Seating Chart Planner

Table #

Table #

Table #

Table #

SEATING PLANNER NOTES:

Seating Chart Planner

Table #

Table #

Table #

Table #

SEATING PLANNER NOTES:

Seating Chart Planner

Table #

Table #

Table #

Table #

SEATING PLANNER NOTES:

Seating Chart Planner

Table #

Table #

Table #

Table #

SEATING PLANNER NOTES:

www.ingramcontent.com/pod-product-compliance
Lightning Source LLC
Chambersburg PA
CBHW080417290526
45791CB00008BA/2308